What Does Hate Look Like?

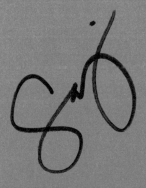

In memory of my mother…who always loved me, advised me, and supported my dreams. To my father…for your never-ending love, support, and cryptic crosswords.

—CP

To Mom and Dad. The strongest people I know. My heroes. To my husband. My biggest supporter. My inspiration.

—SJ

WHAT DOES HATE LOOK LIKE?

SAMEEA JIMENEZ   CORINNE PROMISLOW

with LARRY SWARTZ

Second Story Press

Library and Archives Canada Cataloguing in Publication

Title: What does hate look like? / Sameea Jimenez, Corinne Promislow ; with Larry Swartz.
Names: Jimenez, Sameea, author. | Promislow, Corinne, author. | Swartz, Larry, author. | Neufeld, Juliana, 1982- illustrator.
Description: Illustrated by Juliana Neufeld.
Identifiers: Canadiana (print) 20220390231 | Canadiana (ebook) 2022039024X | ISBN 9781772602906 (softcover) | ISBN 9781772602913 (EPUB)
Subjects: LCSH: Hate—Juvenile literature. | LCSH: Hate—Social aspects—Juvenile literature. | LCSH: Hate speech—Juvenile literature. | LCSH: Hate speech—Social aspects—Juvenile literature.
Classification: LCC HM1166 .J56 2023 | DDC j302.2—dc23

Cover and illustrations by Juliana Neufeld
Edited by Brittany Chung Campbell
Printed and bound in Canada
Designed by Laura Atherton

Second Story Press gratefully acknowledges the support of the Ontario Arts Council and the Canada Council for the Arts for our publishing program. We acknowledge the financial support of the Government of Canada through the Canada Book Fund.

Published by
Second Story Press
20 Maud Street, Suite 401
Toronto, Ontario, Canada
M5V 2M5
www.secondstorypress.ca

TABLE OF CONTENTS

In spite of everything, I still believe that people are really good at heart.

—Anne Frank

In a society where all are related, simple decisions require the approval of nearly everyone in that society. It is society as a whole, not merely a part of it, that must survive. This is the Indigenous understanding. It is the understanding in a global sense. We are all Indigenous people on this planet, and we have to reorganize to get along.

—Rebecca Adamson

Fear of something is at the root of hate for others, and hate within will eventually destroy the hater.

—George Washington Carver

INTRODUCTION

Darkness cannot drive out darkness; only light can do that. Hate cannot drive out hate; only love can do that.

—Martin Luther King, Jr.

We think we know what hate looks, sounds, and feels like, but when you really think about hate, what comes to mind? You might think about broccoli or brussels sprouts or stinky cheese. Or having the flu or a tummy ache. Or maybe you think about your sibling borrowing something that's yours without asking or getting something that you didn't. But none of this is really hate, because hate, when directed at someone or a group of people, creates a big emotional and physical response. The truth is hate is sometimes difficult to put into words and it's hard to understand.

We hear many stories about racism, discrimination, and hate every day. You may be familiar with these incidents from your own life.

You may have encountered hateful events within your community, on social media, YouTube, or in movies. By reflecting on these real-life situations, you can find ways to help deal with what happened to you or offer advice to someone who is affected by the hateful incident.

In this book, children ages eight to fourteen tell their stories of how hate affected them. We explore hatred through kids' eyes and touch on what is hate and how to counter it. This is not intended to be a complete survey of every type of hate that exists: tragically, that would be impossible to fit all in one book. This is intended to show many of the types of hate regularly seen and experienced in classrooms today. Some images and stories in this book might be difficult to see and read. But these stories, along with others, are why we need this book.

WHY WE'VE WRITTEN THIS BOOK

STORIES FROM THE AUTHORS

At the end of Grade 7, we all had autograph books to sign instead of yearbooks. I gave mine to my classmates to sign just like everyone else. Danny G. wrote, "The Year of the Cow." It was so hurtful and humiliating that I didn't want to give the book to anyone else. But Elaine G. grabbed it from my hand, read Danny's comment, and started laughing. I wanted to disappear, to be swallowed up by the ground, or to become invisible. She wrote the same thing. Danny was a mean bully, but I thought Elaine was my friend. I don't think they will ever know how much their words and laughter hurt.

As a Jewish woman who struggled with weight, I have experienced my share of hate and microaggressions. Words and actions are powerful, especially if they still affect you decades later. Being made fun of for not having the "ideal" body affected me long after Grade 7. It becomes a constant reminder that you are different and not acceptable for who you are. And although I may not remember much about Grade 7, I certainly remember the first and last names of the bullies who made me feel like I didn't belong.

Young people are still drawing swastikas on walls in classrooms and doing the Nazi salute. It breaks my heart. Most often, they don't know what they're doing and don't know how much pain and suffering Jewish people endured under the Nazi regime. Or that 6 million Jews (1.5 million of them children) were murdered in the Holocaust just because they were Jewish. Because they were different, they were hated. I'm writing this book to show the pain and suffering caused by hate in all its forms and to offer ideas for how we can advocate for ourselves and become upstanders instead of bystanders.

—Corinne Promislow

A few months ago, a man asked me, "Where did you get that tan from?" The gentleman was surprised when I told him I was Canadian. He responded, "You can't be Canadian if you look like that."

I have felt the effects of hatred from as young as I can remember. My food, culture, and religion have always been questioned and seen as something foreign, something that didn't belong. I instinctively fear the most hurtful question, "Where are you from? No, where are you really from?" when meeting new people. As a

Pakistani Muslim woman who was born and raised in Canada, I was constantly made to feel like I didn't look "Canadian enough." This came from strangers, teachers, and friends. I still experience it regularly as an adult. I know what it feels like to be judged because of the color of your skin, to be hated because of your religion, and to be disliked before someone even gives you a chance to talk. I'm writing this book because I want you to remember you are not alone; we have all experienced hate in different ways. Through this book, I hope we can begin to heal by hearing other people's stories and learn that we don't need to fear what's different; it's these differences that make each of us unique.

—*Sameea Jimenez*

"Larry's a fairy!" Sometimes, some people like to make fun of other people's names. My name is Larry, and I would often hear that taunt in school. I'd cringe knowing I was being mocked because of my behavior. Sometimes these words were said to my face, more often behind my back as I passed by. I hated hearing cruel, anti-gay slurs said about me or about someone else. Why would someone make fun of someone's name? Why would someone make fun of someone's sexuality? When confronted, the tormentor would say, "I was just joking!" I'm writing this book because hate is not a joke. If it's so funny, why am I not laughing?

—*Larry Swartz*

CHAPTER 1

WHERE DOES HATE COME FROM?

No one person is born hating another person because of the color of his skin, or his background, or his religion. People must learn to hate, and if they can learn to hate, they can be taught to love, for love comes more naturally to the human heart than its opposite.

—Nelson Mandela

When you experience hate or see someone so full of rage, it may be hard to believe that hate is not something you are born with. Babies are born loving…they don't see color, race, ethnicity, or religion, they just see people. So, where does it come from and why do people hate?

There is no easy answer to that question.

There are so many potential causes. Often, emotions fuel hatred and they can be difficult to control. Everyone's lives, families, and experiences are different. Whether it's based on your religion, your personal feelings, or what your family or society teaches you, hate is all around us. Sometimes we don't even know it's there.

Because every human is unique, we all view and understand the world in our own way. Having differences is normal and okay, but when you don't take the time to understand and respect what makes us all different, you can become biased toward or against others.

Have you ever felt angry and didn't know why? Or seen someone who was different from you and made a judgment about what they liked and the kind of person they were? Have you ever heard people speaking a different language and thought those people didn't belong? These feelings are normal but being biased can be the beginning of actions and feelings of hate.

Hate is an emotion, a feeling, an action, and a reaction. Hate can be directed at objects, individuals, religions, creeds, groups of people, and, of course, races. Hate can be triggered by ignorance and misinformation. Hate is learned, taught, seen, heard, and felt. It's fear, anger, hurt, and pain. It can come from negative feelings about yourself or others, triggered by jealousy or envy because of other people's status or possessions. Hate can be felt deep inside your mind and body. It stems from bias and prejudice. Hate can be the fear of the unknown or developed when people have power over others. Hate is ignorance and intolerance.

Whether we are the recipient of hate or the person delivering it, hatred creates a tense, uncomfortable feeling in our minds and bodies. When people feel these emotions, it causes your body to react. You know when you are angry, and your body feels tense and stressed and tight? That can turn into hate.

CHAPTER 2

WHAT DOES HATE LOOK LIKE IN REAL LIFE?

Many of us think we know what racism looks like and who the racists are, what parts of the country they live in and the terrible things they think and do. And conveniently enough it's never us. It's always them.

—Krishna Mann

FROM HARMLESS TO HURTFUL SYMBOLS OF HATE

Adolf Hitler was in power from 1933 until the end of World War II in 1945. Hitler was the driving force of the Holocaust, the only purpose of which was to eliminate the Jewish people and anyone else he didn't feel was "pure" through systematic imprisonment and murder. Hitler's Nazi party killed six million Jews, including one and a half million Jewish children. Eleven million people were killed overall. During this era, hate looked like this photo. The raised hand was a salute to Hitler and his ideas that Jewish people and others didn't deserve to be alive because of their religion, political beliefs, ethnicity, or sexual orientation. When others mimic that salute or say "*Heil Hitler*," meaning "Praise Hitler," it is hateful and hurtful. It should never be done.

A hateful salute: Adolf Hitler and the Nazi swastika

Today, the Nazi swastika continues to be a symbol of hate and is used by white supremacists to symbolize their hatred of anyone who is not white or who is considered "other."

Symbols have always been a part of social movements. The raised Black fist has a long history of symbolizing unity, strength, and resistance for Black people and civil rights around the world. White supremacists stole this image and created the raised white fist image to devalue the Black fist symbol and spread hate against people of color. The "OK" hand symbol is commonly used to show something is going well but has now been adopted by white supremacists as a symbol of hate toward people of color. When using this symbol, it is important to think about context; be aware when there may be an underlying meaning of hate and racism. Sometimes just seeing an image can remind people of the hurt and pain caused by a hateful idea associated with it. Pepe the Green Frog was once a harmless, funny meme that has now been appropriated by white supremacists as a symbol of white power. These symbols are extremely hurtful to people of color and anyone else offended by symbols of hate.

Did you know...that in 2020 in Canada, hate crimes against the East Asian, Southeast Asian, and Pacific Islander populations increased by 301%?

The "OK" and raised fist symbols have been adopted by white supremacists

SIGNS OF HATE CRIMES

The words "Death to Islam" and the Nazi swastika are Islamophobic and antisemitic. Often, these words and symbols are drawn on schools, mosques, synagogues, or other cultural gathering places. These words and symbols are hurtful to more than just Muslims and Jews as hate can affect anyone who sees and understands it.

Hateful words and symbols defacing a mosque

Hateful graffiti scribbled on a wall

Graffiti can be a beautiful art form when people express their ideas and emotions through artful words and pictures. But graffiti becomes hateful and harmful when it is used to target or discriminate against a group of people. These are examples of hateful graffiti.

RELIGIOUS ATTACKS AND RELIGIOUS VIOLENCE

Many places of worship have become targets of hate and violence. Specifically, more and more, synagogues and mosques are attacked by intruders who want to harm the people inside. In these attacks, Jews and Muslims have been murdered while they are praying just because of their religion. Antisemitic and Islamophobic graffiti is often painted on synagogue and mosque signs. Have you ever seen words like "go home" or "you don't belong here" on those buildings? Seeing these symbols and words of hate is hurtful and scary.

A woman walks past antisemitic graffiti

Swastika graffiti on a building

Did you know...the Jewish community is the most targeted religious group in the United States?

RACIAL ATTACKS AND RACIAL VIOLENCE

People of color experience hate and violence at much higher rates than white people just because of the color of their skin. For example, Derek Chauvin is a white police officer who was convicted of murdering George Floyd, a Black man, in May 2020. He knelt on Mr. Floyd's neck while Mr. Floyd begged for his life and repeatedly said, "I can't breathe." Why did this happen? Why didn't Chauvin stop when George Floyd said he couldn't breathe? George Floyd was targeted for a crime and arrested, and when he became stressed and afraid, Chauvin physically restrained him even though George Floyd was already in handcuffs. Tragically, after Chauvin knelt on his neck for nine minutes, George Floyd was killed.

Why didn't Chauvin see a man who was afraid? Black people are seen as a threat and are killed by police more than twice as often as white people.

Another example is that since COVID-19 was first detected in Wuhan, China, attacks against Chinese and other East Asian and Pacific Islander peoples have become more common. These groups of people around the world have been unfairly targeted as being responsible for COVID-19. People have been insulted, assaulted on sidewalks, and had buckets of gross things thrown at them because they belong to East Asian, Southeast Asian, or Pacific Islander communities.

The global pandemic has caused huge disruptions to everyone's lives, closing schools and stores, and causing people to lose their jobs.

A demonstration demanding justice for George Floyd

All around the world—including in China and other East Asian countries—people have become sick and have lost friends and family to the pandemic. Millions of people have died from COVID-19. Any one of these experiences is scary and stressful. Sometimes it's easier—even tempting— to blame someone else for your problems.

Did you know...*that in 2020 hate-motivated crimes against the South Asian population increased by 49%?*

It gives you something to be angry at that you can see and touch right in front of you. But no one person, country, or race should be blamed for a global pandemic. Hurting someone will never stop the spread of COVID-19. It only causes more pain.

Fighting back against anti-Asian hate

USING HATE TO INTIMIDATE AND BULLY OTHERS: PHYSICAL, CYBER, VERBAL

Bullying is a form of hate. In this picture, a girl is being excluded and laughed at by her peers. If this has happened to you, you may know how she feels.

Cyberbullying is also a form of hate. Sometimes, people are more likely to say something mean or cruel online because they don't see the victim's reaction. It's easier, because they don't have to watch the impact their words have. But posting hurtful comments online or sending an anonymous message still has impact just like saying it to someone's face. And often, online hatred is more common and persistent because the Internet is public, it isn't limited to your physical community. Online comments follow you home. They sit in your pocket and wait on your screen. Often, victims of cyber-bullying feel like they can't escape it because it is constant and it is everywhere. Saying mean things to or about people on the Internet is hateful and can result in suspension from school.

Physical bullying is a severe form of hate that can have long-term and permanent consequences. Physically hurting someone is dangerous and can result in being arrested for assault and/or suspended from school.

CHAPTER 3

WHAT DOES HATE LOOK LIKE, FEEL LIKE, AND SOUND LIKE IN PICTURES AND REAL STORIES?

The opposite of love is not hate, it's indifference. The opposite of art is not ugliness, it's indifference. The opposite of faith is not heresy, it's indifference. And the opposite of life is not death, it's indifference.

—Elie Wiesel

When you think about hate, what does it sound like? What does it look like in your mind? What does it feel like in your body? Hate can look like anger. Hate is sometimes loud but can also be very quiet. Hate feels scary and stressful. Sometimes, it makes you cry.

The drawings and stories featured were collected from children ages eight to fourteen. The stories, from real children in real situations, reflect their experiences with hate and how it made them feel. The selected drawings represent their imagined or real images of hate. Please note, all names have been changed to protect the identity of the children.

Did you know... *Black Americans remain the most targeted group of all in terms of hate crimes in the US?*

THiS iS WHAT **HATE** *LOOKS* LiKE.

ANTISEMITISM

Antisemitism is prejudice, violence, or hostility toward Jewish people. What does this look like? Jews experience hate through symbols like the Nazi swastika and hurtful language. The swastika is an ancient symbol that is still a sacred symbol in Hinduism, Buddhism, and Jainism. In the 1930s in Germany, when Adolf Hitler and his Nazi party came into power, they appropriated the swastika for their own use. Hitler turned the original symbol on its side and put it on a flag in red and black. This became known as the symbol of the Nazi party and, ultimately, extreme hate. Millions of people were killed in World War II because they were different. Different because of their religion, skin color, sexuality, or their mental or physical disabilities. Six million Jewish people died just because they were Jewish. Almost half a million Roma were murdered because they had darker skin. This type of hate may seem unimaginable, but it still happens today.

Hurtful language used against Jews can suggest they should not exist, and sometimes hurtful language attacks who they are and what they believe. Jewish people are less than 0.5% of the world's population yet remain the most targeted religious group in many countries, including the US and Canada. Jews have been the target of hate crimes that range from name-calling and threats, random violent attacks, racist graffiti, to murders in synagogues. Have you ever seen antisemitic graffiti in your school? Have you ever judged Jewish people based on stereotypes? Is this fair?

Jewish people can be found in every country in every race, but they are judged just because they worship in a different way. And antisemitism is on the rise. Swastikas are drawn in schools every day. Flags with Nazi symbols are still flown at political rallies. These symbols and words are so harmful to Jewish people because they not only trigger survivors who lived through the horrors of the Holocaust but trigger all Jews who see it as a symbol of wanting to destroy Jewish people.

"One day, I walked into my classroom and saw a swastika drawn on the board in marker. I couldn't believe my eyes. My great-grandfather was a Holocaust survivor and had always told me stories of the horror and pain and sorrow he suffered at the hands of the Nazis. The swastika is a symbol of that pain and horror. I can't understand why someone would draw that in my class. I don't think they realize how hurtful it is to me to see that. It makes my heart hurt so much because my great-grandfather passed away last year. His legacy lives on in me and my siblings. His pain is my pain, and his suffering is my suffering. I will not allow his story, his pain, and his survival to be lost or forgotten. Never again."

Did you know...that in 2020 in Canada hate crimes against the Black population increased by 92%?

ANTI-BLACK RACISM

Anti-Black racism is hatred toward Black people. Too often people judge others by the color of their skin. Historically, Black people have been discriminated against solely based on skin color. Within the Black community, we also see racism or discrimination take place in the form of colorism, where darker-skinned people are more discriminated against than people with lighter complexions.

Anti-Black racism is seen in many forms. Verbal attacks, physical and emotional violence, and harmful and hateful words and symbols. The most notorious of the hateful words is the N-word.

The N-word is rooted in deep hatred toward Black people. It is a term that was created in the early 1800s and used by white people during slavery when Black Africans were stolen from their land and held captive against their will. It was a term used to degrade and dehumanize Black people, inherently making whoever said it more superior. The word has since been adopted and said by people as a demeaning, hateful insult toward Black people. The N-word can cause deep emotional harm to people in the Black community and is one of the most harmful words in the English language. The term is so hurtful because it is so closely tied to the suffering Black people have been facing throughout history and continue to face today. Have you ever wondered why Black people can say the N-word and others can't? Black people have reclaimed or taken back the N-word. This means that if you identify as Black, it is your decision on how you would like to use that word, no one else's, especially if that person is not Black. Some Black people use the N-word as a term of endearment and have reclaimed the word to erase its negative connotation. But many other people in the Black community feel like the N-word should never be used as the word still triggers powerful negative emotions.

"My friends and I were at the dollar store shopping on a weekend like we normally do. When we walked in, we saw the two workers stop their conversation and turn to look at us. This didn't bother us. It was when they started following us in the store that really got me mad. Every aisle I went down, the worker would conveniently go down also. I knew right away what was happening. I'm a thirteen-year-old Black boy, I know how the world sees me, they always think I am up to no good. I had ten dollars in my pocket and have never stolen anything in my life. I finally turned to the worker and said 'Are you following me? I'm not going to steal anything, I have money.' He looked at me and said, 'I don't trust N*****s like you.' I have never been called that word before. I still can't describe the pain and anger I felt at that moment. I can't understand how someone could use that word. It is intolerable. Nothing has hurt me as bad as that did. I didn't deserve that."

"It started in third grade. I was and still am a victim of skin shaming. I was friends with this group of girls. There was one girl who hated me. She always made fun of me because my skin was darker than hers. I started to hate the color of my skin and kept saying to myself every day that I hate my skin color. I felt like I was less desirable and less lovable because my skin is darker. I know it's not true, but the pain and embarrassment of hearing her hateful words haunt me to this day."

Did you know..._98% of gay students hear classmates say "that's so gay" or "you're so gay" in school?_

HOMOPHOBIA

Have you ever heard someone or have said yourself "that's so gay" about something weird, unusual, or different? Did you ever wonder why we use that phrase? The term gay used to mean cheerful or happy, but in the 1960s it became associated with homosexual men. To say, "that's so gay," meaning something is bad or weird, is to say that being gay is also bad or weird. And it's not! That phrase is harmful to the members of the 2SLGBTQIPA+ (2 Spirit, Lesbian, Gay, Bisexual, Transgender, Queer or Questioning, Intersex, Pansexual, Asexual, and additional sexual orientations and gender indentities) communities because it makes someone feel that they don't belong.

Did you know..._people who identify as girls or non-binary or gender fluid are more likely than people who identify as boys to be bullied or targeted online?_

"I remember very vividly the first time I was called a homophobic name. I was in my apartment watching YouTube when I heard a knock on the door. Since I was home alone, I went to the door to open it. There was no one there. I closed the door, but before it fully closed a little yellow sticky fell to the ground. On the sticky were the words 'die' and an anti-gay slur written in black marker. I stopped and stared for a moment and didn't know what to do. There was no one in the hallway. I looked up and down several times as tears stung my eyes. Then I heard snickering as the elevator doors closed, and I shut my door and sat on the floor. I sat there for a very long time. The pain was unbearable. I thought people in my building were my friends. I walked to school with them every day. They knew I was gay, and no one had ever made fun of me before. I was devastated. I didn't know how to react. Whoever did that never realized how much those words hurt me. That day changed me forever because a little part of me will never feel good enough again."

ANTI-INDIGENOUS HATE

Anti-Indigenous hate is hatred and hostility toward Indigenous Peoples. Indigenous people and the lands they have lived on for thousands of years have been colonized and occupied for centuries by non-Indigenous people. Historically, colonizing settlers came into countries and assumed they knew the stories of the Indigenous Peoples living there. And they have been telling those stories ever since. This has taken the voice away from its rightful owners, Indigenous Peoples. All Indigenous populations have been affected and some nations have been wiped out by assimilation or elimination. Non-Indigenous people continue to occupy and sell traditional lands and refuse to honor Indigenous Treaties.

Indigenous peoples are still fighting for basic human rights. What can you do to learn more about the territories and lands you live on or where your school is situated? It is only through honoring the right to self-government and Truth and Reconciliation that true healing can begin.

Did you know...*nearly one third of youth identifying with 2SLGBTQIPA+ communities attempted suicide at least once compared to 6% of straight youth?*

Did you know... *the suicide rate among Indigenous youth aged 15–24 is 5 to 6 times the rate seen in the general Canadian population?*

35

"I was in a store walking around looking for my mother. I was 13. We had become separated when she went to look at clothes, and I wandered over to the sports section. I was looking aimlessly at bikes and gears, pressing brake handles, etc. A man walked over and started looking at bikes too. I thought maybe he was waiting for his wife or was looking at bikes, but he kept looking at me. I was starting to feel uncomfortable. I kept taking my phone out of my pocket to see if my mom texted. I did this after looking at the price tag on a bike. The tag fell to the ground. I picked it up and placed it loosely on the handlebars. I put my hands back in my pockets. The man immediately ran over and told me to empty my pockets. An employee heard and came to see what was going on. I said I had nothing in my pockets, just my phone. He immediately got on a walkie-talkie and asked for backup. The employee stood there shaking her head and said, 'These people are the worst! They think they're entitled to everything.' I looked at her in disbelief. The man said, 'Well, they have everything given to them on reserves.' A manager came over and asked what was going on. The man said I stole something off a bike or I was switching price tags. The manager said, 'Take him to the back room and call the police, don't do it here!' Thankfully, my mother came out of nowhere and asked what was going on. The manager said, 'Let's go to the back and talk about this.' My mother was furious and said we were not going anywhere and took out her phone and started filming. She asked me what happened, and I explained about the tag and the man following me and what the man and employee said. My mother looked at them and asked, 'Did you say this?

Did you know...
between 2018 and 2019 the number of police-reported crimes motivated by hatred against race or ethnicity increased 10%?

Did you say this to a thirteen-year-old First Nation boy?' They lied and said they'd said no such thing. My mother was so angry she said to empty my pockets to prove I had nothing. I turned my pockets inside out and two Halls wrappers fell out. I went over and held up the tag on the handlebars. The manager apologized and went to walk away. My mother was not done. She said in a very loud voice, '(The store's name) is full of racism and picks on Anishinaabe people.' The manager asked her to lower her voice, but she wasn't done. She asked the manager to talk to him privately in this back room he'd mentioned, and he nodded yes. We went back there. My mother is a very well-educated, professional woman who explained to the manager the truth of the matter. Both the manager and the store employee were fired. This is only one incident, sadly, since then there have been many."

THiS iS WHAT **HATE** "FeeLS" LiKE.

ISLAMOPHOBIA

Islamophobia is hatred and fear toward the religion of Islam or Muslims. Have you ever seen someone look at a Muslim boy or a girl in a hijab and call them a terrorist? Where does this come from? It comes from stereotypes and biases in news and social media that then become the definition of the religion. These stereotypes are offensive and hurtful. There are not a lot of shows that portray Muslim people in a positive light or at all. Perhaps the first time some of you reading this book ever saw a Muslim person was on TV when they were talking about a terrorist attack. There are more than two billion Muslim people in the world. Muslims are not all the same. Muslim people live in different countries, speak different languages, and wear different

Did you know...
69% of women who wear a hijab have reported at least one incident of discrimination?

types of traditional clothing. Fear makes people think in stereo-types. Fear and ignorance make some people think that all Muslims must be the same.

"I was waiting outside the mosque with my family to go to Friday prayer. A man pulled up in his car, yelling and calling us all terrorists. We ran inside because, just the week before, a mosque had been bombed, and people had died. We heard him yelling for a while. My mom held me close and cried. The fear was overpowering.

My mom was so traumatized, she didn't speak the rest of the day. I still get anxious when we walk to the mosque. I will never understand why people want me to die because of my religion. My mom has never been the same since that day. She just always seems a little sadder than she was before."

ANTI-ASIAN HATE

Anti-Asian hate, which encompasses East Asian, South Asian, and Pacific Islanders, is hatred toward people in Asian communities. The term Asian encompasses a wide range of identities. Many people belonging to the East Asian communities are often identified as Chinese even if they are not. The term Asian is an umbrella term for all peoples living on the continent of Asia. Different countries in Asia have their own language, culture, and traditions. As well, the South Asian communities are very diverse with many different languages, cultures, and religions.

"One day, I was walking down a main city street and this man looked at me and said, 'Go back to China.' I walked toward the nearby park, and he kept following me. I started to run, and he yelled, 'Don't eat my dog!' and kept following me. I ran through the park to a nearby store and tried to lose him, but I couldn't.

My feet started to feel heavy, and my heart was pounding so fast. I was afraid. He was a big man and very intimidating. I finally found a lady to walk next to on the street and pretended I was related to her just so he would leave me alone. She saw the fear on my face and the tears in my eyes and asked if I wanted to call my mom. I called her and could barely speak. When I finally got the story out through sobs, my mom was on her way to pick me up. It was so stressful; I still cry when I think about it."

"I always ride my bike on the path just behind my house. I have for many years and I love it. Ever since COVID-19 happened, some people on the path have treated me differently. They don't let me pass when I want to, or they step in front of my bike like I wasn't there and make me brake hard and almost fall off the bike. One day, I was riding my bike and a teenager was coming at me from the other direction. As we passed by each other, he spat on me. He yelled that I was the reason COVID-19 was here and told me to go back home. This, sadly, was not the first time I had heard that, but I was so upset by being spit on, I stopped riding and got off my bike. It felt paralyzing. Someone had spat on me because I was Chinese. Someone had spat on me, and we were in the middle of a pandemic. Then I got nervous that I might have gotten Covid from his spit. It was so stressful that I couldn't even ride home. I walked my bike back to my house and took a shower as fast as I could. How could someone think that I was the reason for Covid when I have never even been to China? How could I be blamed for a global pandemic just because I am Chinese? Sometimes now I tell people I am Korean just so they won't blame me for the pandemic, but that makes me feel ashamed."

Did you know..._that in 2021, hate crimes in American cities increased by 39%? And hate crimes against Asian Americans increased by more than 200%?_

HOMOPHOBIA

"One day, I was at the community center with my friend. A boy was playing ping-pong wearing plaid pants. My friend looked at him, looked at his pants, and then said, 'Those pants are so gay.' He had no idea that I had been struggling with my sexual identity. He would never know that saying what he said made me feel so ashamed and confused. He was my best friend, and I didn't want to lose that friendship. I was terrified to come out and tell him how I have been feeling; terrified to admit that I was different from what he thought I was. That comment about pants changed our relationship forever. I felt he would never accept me for who I truly was, so I never told him. Sadly, the next year we were in different classes and our friendship was never the same. I wish people would never use the word 'gay' to mean something they think is different or weird. I am gay, I am not bad or weird."

Did you know...
2SLGBTQIPA+ people are targeted for violent hate crimes at a rate of two times that of Muslims or Black people, four times that of Jewish people, and fourteen times that of Latinos?

BODY-SHAMING

Have you ever wondered why society thinks it's okay to comment on people's appearance? We do it all the time. People always think it's a compliment to tell someone how good they look after they lose weight. "You look great! Have you lost weight?" Does that mean you didn't look good before when you were heavier? How do people know you haven't lost weight because you are sick or stressed out? Sometimes people comment on how skinny people are, too. We hear things like, "You have no shape. Where are your muscles?"

or "You're so skinny; I wish I could look like you!" Again, no one knows why someone's body is the way it is and commenting on someone's body size brings attention to how they look rather than who they are. It's an insult, not a compliment. Body-shaming can look like anything that makes someone feel self-conscious about their body. Body-shaming is dangerous as it can cause self-esteem and mental-health problems in children and teens. Everyone is beautiful and no one should be judged on how they look.

Did you know... *that approximately 160,000 teens in the US skip school each year because of bullying?*

"No one's perfect, but people who don't fit the perfect body image laid out by influencers or models can sometimes get bullied. That was the case for me in grades 2 through 5. I wasn't the pretty, skinny girl in any class; my bully was. I was the chubby girl with glasses, and I am okay with it now. My story is something that seems innocent from the outside (this is why it went on for three years), but it's far from it. The bully wasn't hurting me physically, and the teacher never stopped it. She would call me names, leave me out of games, and make me feel useless. And the worst part was I thought we were friends so I couldn't leave. I have never recovered from it. I try to be brave every day but I still feel useless and ashamed because my body is bigger. I feel like I will never be good enough and will never find love. Why would anyone love someone who looked like me? Why is it that body-shaming is still an acceptable form of hurting people? There are people who feel like they can't go to school because of how bad it is for them. The pain of body-shaming stays with you forever."

ABLEISM

Ableism is prejudice against people with disabilities based on the belief that people who do not have disabilities are superior or better. They include people who are blind, deaf, or hard of hearing; physically or mentally challenged; and anyone with a learning disability. Have you ever seen a person with Down syndrome not being able to participate in a talent show? Or someone in a wheelchair refused entry on a school team? Or a blind person being told they can't work at a fast-food restaurant? These are all examples of ableism. Some may believe that people who are disabled need to be changed or that they are considered to be "less than." But every person is enough exactly the way they are.

Did you know..._a third of kids around the world experience hate every year?_

"I always enjoyed going to the community center. I have muscular dystrophy (MD) and my

48

legs don't work as well as others. I can use crutches sometimes, but mostly I am in a wheelchair. At the
community center, they are all really nice to me. But
one day, there was a new person supervising in the gym.
The community center gym is on the second floor, so
I had to walk up the stairs using my crutches and have
someone carry my wheelchair for me. Usually it's no
problem, but that day was a big problem. When I got
to the gym, the kids were picking teams for basketball.
I love basketball. This is the reason I go to the community center—so I can play. The supervisor told me that I
was in the wrong place. He told me to go away. He said
that 'crippled' kids should not be in the gym because
we could get hurt and he could get in trouble. I was so
upset. I couldn't get the words out because my anger
was building up inside me. I wanted to scream. Calling
me crippled was so painful. It hurt me so much because
I can't change the fact that I have MD. I couldn't even
move to leave the gym. One of the boys I know came
over to me. I pushed him away because I was so mad. I
have never been so humiliated and angry in my whole
life. I finally wheeled to the middle of the gym and told
the supervisor to go to hell. I picked up a basketball,
scored a shot from the three-point line, and wheeled
away. I have never gone back because I never want to
experience that pain again."

THIS IS WHAT HATE SOUNDS LIKE.

ANTISEMITISM

"It happened in Grade 8 French class. The teacher left the room and three boys stood up and did the Hitler salute to our teacher. One yelled '*Heil Hitler*' when she came back into the room. The teacher was so shocked and tears welled up in her eyes. She is an older lady who is Jewish. Someone told us later that her parents survived the Holocaust. I really liked her, she was a great teacher, and it made me angry and sad that these boys did this and made her feel this way. No one deserves that."

ANTI-BLACK RACISM

"So, I was hanging out with my friends at the mall one day. We were just chilling and having fun. Then a bunch of white girls come by and start getting in our business. We told them to leave us alone. Then one of the girls shouts, 'Shut up N*****.' I started to cry but held my tears so she couldn't see that she hurt me, but it hurt so much and I kinda didn't even know why. I don't know why she was that angry, but no one should ever be called that word, ever. I never understood the power of hate behind that word until that moment. I will never forget the first time I was called the N-word sadly knowing it would not be the last."

"I was at the park playing in the wading pool with my dad. There were a couple kids playing, and I waded over and asked if I could play with them. I got no response, so I walked a bit closer. Still, I got no response. I thought that was weird. I asked again even louder and still no response. Then I realized they were ignoring me, and I felt a pit in my stomach. I summoned up the courage to ask one more time, just to be sure. Finally, one of the kids shouted back, 'No! We're not allowed to play with you because you're Black. My mom said no Black friends.' Tears instantly welled up in my eyes. I couldn't breathe and I could barely speak. I slowly walked away feeling humiliated. I tried to be brave, but the tears wouldn't stop, and my dad came over and hugged me tight. This would be the first of many hateful situations I would find myself in because of my skin color."

ISLAMOPHOBIA

"One time, my mom and I (who identify as Muslim and wear a hijab) were taking the subway, and this man walked up to us. The man said, 'Go back to your country!' My mom and I were in such shock because this had never happened to us before. The man got closer and even tried to hit my mom. We felt so threatened and scared. My mom yelled at him in Arabic and then screamed for help. No one came to help; they all just ignored us. I felt invisible. All of this happened because I am Muslim and wear a hijab. I will always wear my hijab with pride, but now know that I am a target because of it."

XENOPHOBIA

Xenophobia is the fear of strangers or people from other countries. Although they overlap, Xenophobia is different from racism because it is the fear of all foreigners and their customs. Xenophobia is often found within the white supremacist movement. White supremacists feel that their country should represent and reflect their colonial belief system. They feel that anyone who doesn't look like them or agree with their belief system is not welcome in their country.

Did you know... *immigrant-born youth in wealthy countries are more likely to experience hate than locally born youth?*

BODY-SHAMING

"There were two boys that were always bothering my friend at school. They'd sit near us at lunch and tell my friend she was ugly, a fat pig, and many other mean things to make fun of her body. One of the boys had an assigned seat next to me and would talk about my friend, and sometimes even said he would hurt her. The bullying never got physical, which some people said was good, but all those words hurt her a lot. The bullying became so bad she started skipping meals.

She told me that she hated her body and she hated herself. She felt she wouldn't be accepted until she was thin. She developed an eating disorder and got really sick. I don't know why they couldn't accept my friend for who she is, not what she looks like. It makes me so angry that my friend got sick because of ignorant boys and their hateful words."

CHAPTER 4

HOW DO WE MAKE SENSE OUT OF FEELINGS THAT DON'T MAKE SENSE?

MICROAGGRESSIONS

Don't ever think that just because you do things differently, you're wrong.

—Gail Tsukiyama

The stories shared in this book of different ways people have been hurt are hard to read. They may have made you feel icky or reminded you of a time someone said something to you that made you feel this way. Or maybe something you witnessed that just didn't feel right in your body but you weren't sure why. Maybe you still aren't. There are things people say, often unintentionally, that aren't meant to be hurtful but are. These actions can seriously harm individuals and worse still, they often go unaddressed. These are called microaggressions.

Sometimes people don't even know they are doing it. Have you ever heard or said something to someone innocently but the person was offended? Have you ever wondered why? Sometimes a joke or a comment that seems innocent can be really hurtful. If you are offended, then it is up to you to speak up and tell the person why. If someone doesn't *know* it's hurtful, they will continue to *be* hurtful.

Sometimes the world doesn't even know that it's doing it. Is it okay that most bandages only look like white people's skin? A person with darker skin can feel self-conscious about wearing a bandage while no one would know if a white person was wearing one, because it mostly disappears on their skin. Thankfully, this is beginning to change, but in a lot of places, especially in small towns and rural communities, beige bandages are the only ones you can purchase. And even with these changes, there are still challenges. The boxes of bandages for people of color have several shades combined all in one box. This means that people of color can only use a few of the bandages from each box that match their skin tone. Why are there several shades of bandages combined in one box for people of color? What message is that sending?

Is it okay that a lot of crayons do not have colors that match every skin tone? Have you looked and been able to find your skin tone easily? How often do you find one that matches your skin tone? Every box contains a crayon that matches white skin. Many companies have now begun to create boxes that contain all skin tones, but like bandages, those are often only available in big cities. How do you think it would make someone feel if they couldn't find their skin tone to create a self-portrait? How would you feel? It could make someone think their skin tone was not as valid, which we know is not true.

Have you ever wondered why we get all the Christian holidays off school and not any other religions'? How do you think it would feel if you needed to miss school to celebrate your traditions and religious holidays? What if you were missing something fun or important in school? How do you think it feels for someone to have to choose between school and their religion? It can make someone feel like their celebrations are not as important, or somehow less than others'.

Did you know...
Black and Hispanic students are more likely to experience hate in school than their white peers?

All these feelings of being left out, less than, or excluded, fall under the umbrella of something called systemic racism. This is racism or discrimination that is rooted in the systems we all live under. Everyday things that we may not even notice. All these small ways we're told we don't belong or aren't as important as someone else affects how we think and feel. We often talk about hate in words and actions rather than hate that is embedded in our everyday lives.

RACISM

"I usually wear my hair in braids. I took out my braids one night to wear my hair natural for a few days before I got it braided again. At school, when I walked into class, the teacher ran over to me and was like, 'Oh my gosh, your hair is so big! Can I touch it?' It made me feel so uncomfortable. Why do people think it's okay to touch Black girls' hair? It is such an invasion of my personal space and body. I would never ask a girl, or my teacher, to touch their hair!"

"I remember, I was in Grade 5, and we were talking about different holidays in our class. Our teacher started talking about Eid and asked me to explain to the class how my family celebrates. I am Sikh. Sikhs are not Muslim. I felt embarrassed and upset. I really didn't want to explain this again to my peers. Too often I am mistaken for Muslim because of my skin color. I have nothing against the Muslim people, but my religion is different and unique. It made me feel like my teacher was ignorant of my religion. How can I feel safe if no one knows who I am? I felt invisible."

Did you know..._more than half of Sikh children in US schools endure bullying with over two thirds of turbaned Sikh children among the most common victims?_

"In Grade 2, we had a math test one day and I did not do well on the problem question, and my teacher said she was surprised. I asked her why she was surprised, and she said because I was Chinese, and I should be good at math. That was the most insulting thing a person can say. That is such a stereotype and people should be more aware that not everyone fits a stereotype. I was so upset and self-conscious every time we did math in class. It was so disturbing that I got anxiety around math and still get anxious every time I have a math test."

"I remember it was a Friday afternoon at school. I was hanging out with some friends during recess. I was having so much fun with them that I asked if they wanted to come over to my house on the weekend and hang out. The one girl who I thought was my friend said, 'I don't think my dad will drop me off that far.' I was so confused and told her I didn't live far away. She said, 'Oh, I thought all Indigenous people lived on the reserves.' My first reaction was shock. Was my friend that ignorant about my culture? I had known her for two years and couldn't believe how painful and intolerable her reaction was. I looked her straight in the eye and said, 'I live four blocks away from you, but you are no longer invited over.' I went home and cried. I wasn't surprised that people were ignorant of Indigenous Peoples; I just thought a friend would know better."

"I never felt more hurt than when we were asked to talk about our families and family tree and present in front of the class. To give you a background, my parents were born in Somalia, but my sister and I were born in Canada. As I was explaining this to the class, a girl at the back of the room shouted out, 'How can you be born in Canada? Your skin is so dark. Are you sure you weren't born in Somalia too?' Most of the kids started laughing. I felt so embarrassed and angry. Who is she to question where I was born? It was so insulting! Why do people assume that just because I have dark skin, I wasn't born in Canada? It's infuriating that I have to explain who I am every time someone asks, 'But where are you *really* from?'"

"I am lucky because I come from several different backgrounds. But people often get confused when they meet me. My mother is Jewish, born in New York City. I was also born in New York City. I grew up with my mom and my grandmother, who immigrated from Poland. My father is Puerto Rican and Mohawk. I grew up in Brooklyn. My skin is brown, but I look more Indigenous than Latino. My passion is dance. One time at a dance recital, I was talking to my grandmother about my solo dance. When I speak to her, my New York accent comes out and I use Yiddish words. A parent inter-rupted me and asked me how I knew those words. I told her I was Jewish and introduced her to my grandmother. She looked at me funny and said she didn't understand. She just kept looking at me like I was some alien. She was so rude! My grandmother finally had to intervene and say that my father was not white. The woman said 'Oh, I understand,' but I don't think she really did. I have never felt angrier in my life. I wanted to lash out, but my grandmother stopped me. How dare she question who I am because of my skin color!? The Jewish religion is every race... we are more than white. We are Black, Brown, Asian, Latino, Indigenous, and mixed...like me. I am so tired of explaining who I am because I don't fit people's ste-reotypes or their expectations of who I should be."

Did you know... *that in 2020 in Canada, hate crimes against the Indigenous population increased by 152%?*

"My mom cooks the best food. I always used to look forward to my lunches until that was ruined in Grade 4. One day in the cafeteria, I opened my thermos and the boy sitting next to me yelled so loud, 'Eww, your food smells so gross! What are you eating?!' Then, a girl sitting across from me said, 'Your food doesn't look normal. I can't believe you're eating that.' I was so self-conscious and embarrassed but I laughed along because I didn't want them to know that it bothered or hurt me. I threw out my food and didn't eat that day. I went home and was so angry at my mom for putting that food in my lunch. I can never really forgive those people for making me feel ashamed of who I am and where I come from based on my food. Food is so important to my family and my culture and that was taken away from me because of hateful, ignorant people. I am still so insecure about my lunches and how people will judge me because of my food."

"I am Sri Lankan and my name is Aakithya. I was named after my grandmother. I love my name because it reminds me of my grandmother's strength and love. My teachers always have difficulty saying my name. In the middle of the year, we got a new teacher because our teacher had a baby. On the new teacher's first day, we played a 'get to know you' game. When it came to me to introduce myself, the new teacher, in front of the entire class, asked me to repeat my name. Then she asked if I had a nickname, or if she could call me something else because my name was too difficult to pronounce. I was so uncomfortable and embarrassed. I didn't know what to say. I just sat in my seat and cried. This hadn't happened with my regular teacher. She asked me how to pronounce my name and she learned it the first day. This teacher told me to go to the office because I wouldn't stop crying. I sat in the office and cried. I was ashamed of crying and angry that she made me feel this way. I started thinking of nicknames the teacher could call me so it would be easier for her to pronounce my name. I was fearful that the next time I was in class, she would ask me again for my nickname or mispronounce my name and everyone would laugh at me. How was she allowed to humiliate me with her words? How does a teacher not understand how important a name is to a person?"

> **Did you know...**
> *2SLGBTQIPA+ youth experience three times more discrimination than straight youth?*

ISLAMOPHOBIA

"I was on the bus with my friends going to the mall. Out of nowhere, an older man turned around and asked me why I was wearing a hijab? He said, 'I've always been curious to know what you all are hiding under there.' He wasn't trying to be mean or anything; I think he really thought I was hiding something. I tried to ignore him, but it made me feel embarrassed and humiliated. Everyone heard him. I wanted to disappear. Why do people think it's okay to ask me about my clothes? My hijab is my connection to my religion and his questions made me feel naked."

TRANSPHOBIA

"It was the beginning of Grade 7 in a new school. I was excited to be there as I could now be the me I have always known I was meant to be. I was in my homeroom, and we had a supply teacher. The teacher was doing attendance and called out the name 'Emily.' He said it again, and when no one responded he said, 'Emily Crawford.' I could hardly breathe. Someone next to me said, 'Isn't your last name Crawford?' I ran out of the room crying. I had so wanted to start fresh in a new school, and now everyone knew, and I felt judged again. I called my mom, and she called the school. She told the school to change my name to Theo because that is my name. The secretary asked me 'But what is your *real* name?' I went home that day and never went back. I changed schools and started as Theo. My real name. I feel so lucky to have a mom who was so supportive of me. It keeps me surviving this journey. Some trans kids are not as lucky as I am. And some trans kids don't survive."

BODY-SHAMING

"I was born a chubby baby and never stopped being chubby. I guess it was cute when I was a baby, but when I got older, everyone would say things to me. My mom and my sister are both skinny—I mean model skinny. People would always tell me to lose weight so I could be like them. They can wear any clothes they want and they look great no matter what, but I feel like I look great the way I look too. My Aunt Ellen is the same as my mom. One day, we all decided to go shopping. Aunt Ellen took me to get new jeans. I tried on one pair, and they fit great. I ran to show my Aunt Ellen. Before I could say anything, she said to me, 'Those are nice jeans for a big girl, but you have such a pretty face, if only you would lose some weight you could fit into skinny jeans and be beautiful.' I felt so humiliated and embarrassed. I was so happy with my jeans and now I couldn't wait to take them off. Aunt Ellen was trying to get me to lose weight with that comment, but all it made me want to do was eat chocolate cake and cry. Why couldn't she just love me the way I am?"

ANTISEMITISM

"I was meeting a group of classmates to work on a group presentation. They know me as Sara Abbott as that's my name on Instagram. My full name is Sara Abbott Goldstein, but it was already taken on Insta. When we were putting names in the Google Doc, I put in Sara Goldstein. One of the girls said, 'I thought your name was Sara Abbott.' I told her that's my mom's last name; my dad's last name is Goldstein. She said, 'That sounds really Jewish.' I told her I am Jewish. She said, 'You don't look Jewish; you have such a small nose.' I was shocked and disappointed and frankly spitting mad. Was that supposed to be a compliment? That my nose was small, so I don't look Jewish? So, do all Jewish people have big noses? How can someone so intelligent in so many areas be so stupid and ignorant and stereotypical!? I couldn't speak and honestly didn't know what to say. I made an excuse to leave and told them I would work on the project from home. I left her house so angry and confused. I didn't know why I was so angry, but I was. I wanted to break something or punch something. It was so infuriating."

KEEP LISTENING TO EACH OTHER

These children were very brave to share their stories and illustrations of hate. It is difficult for anyone to relive these feelings and emotions, but they felt it was necessary to have their voices heard if it could save one person from experiencing what they went through. We know how powerful it is to share stories and to hear other children's experiences so that you can gain a deeper understanding of the pain that exists today. Perhaps you have gone through something like this, or perhaps you recognize things you have said in these stories and are better understanding the impact your words had on the people you said them to.

Whatever experiences you come to this book with, it is important to understand how hate hits. Hate comes from complicated emotions like fear, anger, and sadness, and it causes those same emotions in others. Hate is a complicated web, and it doesn't make anyone feel less alone. The only way we can do that is to better understand each other's differences and all of our similarities.

It is important to learn about other people's experiences and to have empathy when you see someone being hurt. We hope that knowing about these stories will help make your pain easier to bear. Standing with each other, listening, and supporting others can be a strong message that hate will not be tolerated.

CHAPTER 5

HOW DO WE MOVE FROM BYSTANDERS TO UPSTANDERS?

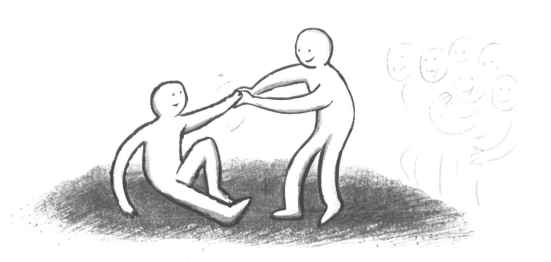

Hate, it has caused a lot of the problems in this world, but has not solved one yet.

—Maya Angelou

So, why should we care? If hate is not happening to you, why should you intervene? Hate can happen to anyone at any time. If you don't stand up against hate today, who will stand up for you tomorrow? It is your responsibility as the future of your community and your country to help stop the pain and suffering caused by hate. It is no longer an option to stand by and watch while others experience hate. As responsible citizens, you need to stand up and speak out against hate and microaggressions in all forms. Now is the time to move from being a bystander to an upstander.

A word of caution: Sometimes you may feel uneasy or unsure of standing up to hate. If you feel scared or are in a situation where you might get hurt, you should leave and ask an adult to help you. You should never put yourself in a situation where you could get hurt. But if you know you won't get hurt and you could help the person who is the victim of hate, then you should stand up for them, because you would want them to stand up for you.

HERE ARE FIVE WAYS YOU CAN STAND UP TO HATE:

1. EDUCATE YOURSELF

One of the best things you can do to combat hate is to educate yourself. Learn and understand from people who are different from you. Learn about different races, religions, sexual orientations, abilities, food, cultures, and communities. We move through the world in our own perspective, and sometimes it is hard to understand that people have different experiences from our own. Often, we fear things we do not understand and make judgments or form opinions based on what we have heard on social media or from family or friends. You have an obligation to learn and understand differences because you would want the same respect shown to you and your feelings, opinions, and beliefs. Get in the habit of asking questions rather than assuming. Get in the habit of being positively curious about other people. Education is an important way to stop hate in our communities.

2.   SPEAK UP

What would you do if...
someone in your school called out a homophobic slur every time you passed each other in the hallway, and you heard giggling as they walked away?

If you witness acts of hate, speak up. Tell an adult or someone who can help you, especially if the situation feels unsafe. Find a balance between courage and caution. When you speak up against injustice and acts of hate, you are not only helping the other person, but you are helping yourself become a stronger advocate for change in the world. When you hear a slur or racist joke, speak up. Do not remain silent in the face of oppression. Even if someone says they are joking, speak up and remind them that racist jokes or jokes making fun of people are hurtful, hateful, and not funny.

One strategy is if you see someone being victimized by hate, try to engage with them in a positive way. This act can help with changing the experience from negative to positive for the victim. For example, if someone calls somebody inappropriate, hurtful names, you could approach the victim and talk to them. If you don't know them, introduce yourself and take them out of the situation, somewhere safe, or to find an adult that can help you. You could invite them to come play with you in another area of the schoolyard or community or start a conversation taking away the attention from the person causing harm. The main idea is to take the focus off the person or people that are causing harm while making the victim feel safe. When this happens, the power shifts from the person who is inflicting harm and moves to the victim. Follow this advice only if you feel safe enough to do so. Otherwise, find a trusted adult who can assist you.

3.   ASK FOR HELP WHEN YOU NEED IT

If you don't understand something, it is okay to ask questions. No one expects you to know it all and be an expert. Growing and learning is something that we never stop doing and the best way to learn is by asking questions. If you are experiencing hate, ask for help. You deserve to feel safe and secure in your school and community. No one should make you feel scared or ashamed because of who you are. Ask for help from your peers, your teachers, your parents, guardians, or religious leaders. There are a lot of people who are willing to support you and willing to stand up for you...you just have to ask.

4.   JOIN FORCES

Educating yourself about others is very important. But education is only the beginning. To stop

What would you do if...
you were walking home from school and you saw someone spray-painting a piece of graffiti that is considered offensive?

77

What would you do if...
you received an email that said something racist about one of your friends?

hate and begin to make change in yourself and for others, you need to make connections with people who are different from you. You have the power to stop hate in your school and community. You don't have to stop hatred on your own. There are so many people around you who can support you and the changes that you can make. Be an ally and look for allies in your school, through clubs and teams, peers, and teachers. You can join clubs outside of school, places of worship, libraries, or community centers. Just because you can make a difference on your own, know that there is strength in numbers. Having allies and joining forces help to strengthen the message you want to share and provides a safe space for you to make change.

5. DIG DEEPER

What does it mean to "dig deeper?" Digging deeper means to challenge your own ideas and views about others. When you see someone who is different from you, do you immediately make assumptions about them? Do you jump to a conclusion when you see a person of a different race, ability, or religion? What are your first impressions? How can you put those first impressions away and get to know someone without judging them based on what you think you know about them? This is called "challenging your bias" or "digging deeper into yourself."

It's hard to acknowledge and accept that you might be the person causing hurt and harm to others. If you are that person, you need to dig deeper inside yourself to figure out why you feel this way. Where is the hate coming from? Confide in a trusted adult that can help you understand your feelings. A trusted adult is someone who will listen to you and help you manage your anger and fear. Just because your thoughts and actions might be hateful or hurtful today doesn't mean this defines who you truly are. You always have the power to challenge your biases and change your thinking.

Digging deeper into yourself also means understanding and being aware of your own privilege. Privilege refers to certain advantages and benefits people have in society. Having privilege is having power. A lot of people have privilege, but it's not always based on skin color. People with power, wealth, education, and opportunity have privilege. White people do have privilege. Just as men, people with money, able-bodied people, straight people, and thin people do. With this privilege comes power and it is important to acknowledge it, if you have it, and use your privilege in a positive, supportive way. It is important that we continue to dig deeper into our learning and understanding to challenge our thinking.

What would you do if...
you heard someone telling a racist joke?

> **What would you do if...**
> your cousin told you he got bullied because he wore nail polish?

REAL STORIES OF HOW TO BECOME AN UPSTANDER

"I was out for lunch with some of my best friends. We are always joking around and laughing together. One of my friends said a racist joke about Chinese people, and the group started laughing. I didn't think it was funny but didn't want to be the only one not laughing. It sat in the pit of my stomach the whole day, and I hated that I didn't say something. I called her later to tell her I don't think it's funny when she says those types of jokes. It wasn't funny to make racist jokes, and that she could really hurt someone's feelings. She didn't say much then, but I never heard her make racist jokes after that. I think she understood."

"I have always been an outgoing person. In Grade 7, I sang a song in front of the whole school for the welcome-back BBQ. Everyone thought I was a very secure person, but I was hiding my truth. I was born female, but I truly felt that I was male. I know what people say about trans people. I know how they are bullied and made fun of. I have heard the jokes and cringed when I heard them. But I didn't want anyone to know my secret. I was afraid that my friends would leave me and that I would be alone. In Grade 8, I met another student who was transitioning from female to male. They were also scared, confused, and felt alone. When they started dressing differently and asked people to call them by a different name, they got bullied and teased. I knew I had to take a stand not just for myself, but for my friend and for anyone else going through this, or anyone who knew someone going through this. At our 'Pink Day' assembly for anti-bullying and 2SLGBTQIPA+ rights, I stood up in front of everyone and introduced myself using my new chosen name. I explained to the whole school that I now consider myself male, that I am transitioning and not fully transitioned. I talked about the dangers that trans people face and asked for their understanding and acceptance. I got a standing ovation

> **What would you do if...**
> you were in a store with your friends and you overheard a customer making fun of the cashier's accent?

> **What would you do if...**
> you arrived at school and noticed that someone had painted a swastika on a locker near yours?

from my peers and teachers. It felt so amazing to be validated and accepted for who I truly am."

"There was a girl in my class that no one seemed to like. I don't know why they didn't like her. I'm guessing it was because she just moved to Canada and didn't speak English as well as the rest of our class. I just went along with it because that's what everyone else was doing. Over time, I noticed she was always last to get picked or never in a group at all during group work. She seemed so sad. One day, we were asked to pick partners, and I finally went up to her and asked if she wanted to be mine. She was so happy! She was so friendly, and I remember laughing so much with her. I told my

> **What would you do if...**
> a boy in your class who used a wheelchair was often excluded from participating in gym class or other class events?

other friends about how nice she was. I started including her more, especially at recess when everyone was playing. We are still friends, and she seems so much happier. I couldn't believe we weren't friends sooner."

CHAPTER 6

WHY SHOULD WE CARE?

When you learn something from people, or from a culture,
you accept it as a gift, and it is your lifelong commitment
to preserve it and build on it.

—Yo-Yo Ma

At the very beginning of this book we asked you what you hated. Now we want to ask you why is it important to learn about hate. Real hate: hate that hurts, hate that is dangerous, and hate that can and will change lives and the world in a bad way. The hate that you have been learning about throughout this book.

We are seeing more and more hate in the world. People don't want to be suffering but they are. Suffering because of the way they're treated based on their race, religion, culture, the color of their skin, their gender identity, abilities, or the size and shape of their bodies. What can you do to make positive change? You can learn about your own bias. Bias can be formed when people discriminate between people who are like them, and not like them. On the good side of bias, you can gain a sense of identity and safety

What would you do if...
you witnessed someone making fun of a girl wearing a hijab?

and belonging. However, more often, bias can lead into an "us" versus "them" mentality.

Sometimes, an "us" versus "them" mentality brings people together and sometimes it can lead to hate. For example, in sports, we cheer for our countries in the Olympics or World Cup. It doesn't matter where the athletes came from, their ethnicity, their religion, or anything else; if they are representing our country, we are proud when they win because we feel they won for us. We belong to the winning team. We are proud when our flag is raised and our national anthem is sung. And we don't cheer for our biggest rival countries.

But within our own countries, we cheer for our city, and we don't cheer for another. For example, when Canada beats the United States in hockey, Canadians cheer for the Canadian team. But when the Toronto Maple Leafs play the Montreal Canadiens, we cheer for our favorite team and against the rival team. *Within* our cities, we cheer for the team we live closest to, like when the New York Yankees play the New York Mets, people from New York choose sides.

These kinds of "us" versus "them" are mostly harmless fun. We feel a strong sense of belonging to our countries on the world stage and that strong sense of belonging to our individual cities when we play *within* our countries.

But when "us" versus "them" translates to people's individuality, meaning who they are, where they came from, what they look like, how and who they love, or how they express their spirituality, it becomes problematic. Like when Jews and Muslims have conflict based on religion, or white people dislike Black people based on their skin color. Or when religious people and people from the 2SLGBTQIPA+ community differ on who to love and the definition of family.

We can't translate our devotion to a team and "hatred" of the rival team to people who are different. That perceived hatred sneaks its way into our minds and creates bias and prejudice. It sometimes happens without our even knowing it, because it has been shown to us in the media, through books, and even hearing family conversations, and in the culture around us.

Do you immediately have an opinion of someone before getting to know them? How often have you said to a person once you got to know them, "You are so different from what I thought you would be?" Or have you ever seen a character in a movie or show and assumed they were the "bad guy" based on their skin color? Or have you ever seen a person with a larger body and assumed they were lazy, unhappy, and unhealthy?

What would you do if...
an immigrant family moved into your neighborhood and neighbors put up a sign on the front lawn saying, "Go home!"?

87

Making an assumption like "all Italians like pasta" takes away individual stories, personalities, likes, and dislikes. Everyone has the right to tell their own story. You have the right to tell your own story. Stories are where we learn about each other and what makes us unique.

> **What would you do if...**
> you saw someone in the washroom who was really upset because someone made fun of the lunch they were eating? You volunteered to help, but the person refused.

CHAPTER 7

WHAT DOES ALL THIS MEAN FOR YOU?

Our greatest glory is not in never falling, but in rising every time we fall.

—Confucius

How can you learn from these stories? How can you connect with your similarities and learn from differences? Listen and be interested in what is different and what is the same between you and your friends and the people in your community. You could be missing out on getting to know someone, having great friendships, or just being more understanding and respectful.

We are not suggesting that you have to be friends with everyone you meet. But we are asking that you don't pass judgment or make snap assumptions based on what you see or hear or feel. Everyone wants to belong. Whether it is a family, a religion, a team, a school, a group of friends, or a community, belonging is at the heart of being human. Connecting is important because it impacts your physical, emotional, and mental health. But if we all belong to our own separate groups and don't get to know each other, we begin to believe hateful stories and buy into stereotypes, which feed our bias and creates hate.

Many of you reading this book may live in communities where everyone looks the same as you or may practice the same religion. This book is especially important for you because, if you don't have anyone in your community to learn from, the courageous people in this book have graciously shared their stories so that you can learn from them. Now that you have the knowledge, you can be and do better.

Hate is growing stronger in our communities and our schools, and education is one of the most powerful ways to combat and overcome hate. This book has highlighted for you some real stories from students about hate and how it has affected real people. Learning, understanding, and respecting differences is the avenue to eliminating hate.

Fear can be the driving force behind hate. You need to overcome your fear of the unknown and be courageous. When you fear something, it's easier to hate than to work through your fear. But working through your fear will free you to be a better, kinder, person. Recognizing what you fear is the first step in overcoming it.

In the meantime, we encourage you to stand up against hate. We have to look past our differences to find our similarities. You should stand up for other people's differences so that one day, someone will stand up for what makes you unique. You have the power with

What would you do if...
your best friend told you
that someone made fun of
their skin color?

your voice and your actions to stop hate and microaggressions and make a positive change in your school, your community, and the future. Big changes start with small moves. And it all begins with you.

WHAT IF YOU HAVE BEEN THE VICTIM OF HATE?

HOW TO COPE

If you have been the victim of hate, reading the stories here may have been very difficult. Some of what you read in this book may have made you think about your own experiences differently. Maybe you've realized that something that happened to you that you dismissed as not intentional or "not a big deal" was in fact harmful. We are often told—by society, and even by our family and friends—to "be brave" or to ignore others' behavior toward us. This might be what you feel most comfortable with or be the safest option for you. Whatever the case, the impact on your mental health can be deep. If you can, seek out help or counseling if it is available.

ASK FOR HELP

If you have been the victim of hate or experienced any of the scenarios in this book, first know that it is not your fault and you have not done anything wrong. Your first action should be to speak to a trusted adult and get the support you need to work through your trauma. Confiding in an adult can also stop the hate from continuing to happen. If you don't have a trusted adult to speak to, you can call a kids help phone, kids help line, or teen crisis line in your community. Experiencing hate can be traumatic. The most important thing to do is to get support for yourself and to keep yourself safe.

HOW TO REACT TO HATE

Here is a checklist that can help you whether you are the victim of, the bystander to, or the person causing hate.

For Victims

- try to stay calm
- tell them to stop or, if it is safer, say nothing
- walk away…if you need to run, RUN
- tell a trusted adult (teacher, coach, parent, guidance counselor, religious leader)

- avoid areas where you don't feel safe in your neighborhood or school
- spend time with people who make you feel good about yourself
- cut ties or avoid people who make you feel bad about yourself
- when you are upset that someone has hurt you, don't respond in anger as it can make the situation worse and you may become the one who causes anger and hurt
- if the hate is happening online, take screenshots and delete accounts and let a trusted adult know
- do not respond to online comments
- call a kids or teen crisis hotline if you feel you have no one to talk to

For Upstanders

- don't ignore the hate incident
- use your voice not your hands to stop the situation
- stand beside the victim for support
- if it is safe to do so, lead the victim away from the situation
- call a kids or teen crisis hotline if you feel you have no one to talk to

For the People Who Inflict Hate

- think about how you would feel if someone did this to you
- consider your victim's feelings

- understand your bias and how that affects the situation
- look inside yourself to understand why you are angry because perhaps your anger is based on something that has nothing to do with the target
- talk to a trusted adult or a kids or teen crisis hotline for help

STATISTICS

The following are hate-crime statistics from various countries recorded by police over the past few years. These statistics are reported by an international human rights organization called the ODIHR (Office for Democratic Institutions and Human Rights):

TYPES OF **HATE**	STATISTICS BY **INCIDENT** — ● Violent attacks against people / ● Threats / ● Attacks against property			TOTAL **INCIDENTS**
RACIST AND XENOPHOBIC	1,212	290	883	2,385
ANTISEMITIC	582	587	1,153	2,322
ANTI-LGBTQ	739	352	117	1,207
ANTI-CHRISTIAN	57	60	881	977
ANTI-MUSLIM	67	89	177	333
GENDER-BASED	140	49	19	208
ANTI-ROMA	48	18	18	84
ANTI-DISABILITY	19	7	3	29
OTHER BASED ON RELIGION OR BELIEF	7	1	4	12

PHOTO CREDITS

Pages 11, 13 - Shutterstock

Page 14 - Courtesy of CAIR (Council on American-Islamic Relations)

Page 15 - Photo by Andrew Lichtenstein, Getty Images

Page 16 - Photo by Philippe Merle, Getty Images

Pages 17, 19, 20, 21, 22, 23 - Shutterstock

ACKNOWLEDGMENTS

This book would not have been possible without the contribution and support of many people, as well as the numerous meaningful conversations, suggestions, and ideas that led to its completion.

The idea for this book came from a conversation with Shari Schwartz-Maltz, Manager of Media and Issues for the Toronto District School Board. Her experience with the stories of hate within the board sparked the concept for this book. For this, we are forever grateful.

This book could not have been written without the contributions of the numerous students who submitted their stories and artwork. Thank you to the students across Canada and the United States who were brave enough to share their most intimate experiences with hate. Even though all your stories and illustrations did not make it into the book, we know how difficult it was for you to put them on paper, and we are eternally grateful.

A huge thank you to Margie Wolfe, who started this journey with us and guided us along the way. Your insights and experience were invaluable. And breakfast was always delicious!

Special thanks to Gillian Rodgerson for always being there when we need you and for always supporting us and our ideas. And thanks to Jordan Ryder for your eagle eye in editing and for bringing us to the finish line. Also special thanks to Emma Rodgers for handling our many email requests with patience and grace. And of course, huge thanks to the rest of the amazing team at Second Story Press…you continued to impress us and always ensured we had what we needed even when we didn't know we needed it.

Thanks to our incredible illustrator, Juliana Neufeld, for your brilliant illustrations throughout the book. They captured exactly what we envisioned and made the book and the stories exponentially better.

Thank you to our editor Brittany Chung Campbell for your deep understanding on why this book was so important. Thank you for your guidance, knowledge, and advice through some of the challenging content and for taking the time to help us with organizing our ideas.

Thank you to Marty Wilson-Trudeau and Phoenix Wilson for your support and guidance in ensuring that Indigenous voices were heard and honored.

Finally, thank you to our families. We appreciate and love each and every one of you and could not have done this without your support!